LAWYERS OF DISTINCTION

DISTINGUISH YOURSELF

Copyright © 2018. All Rights Reserved.

No part of this publication may be reproduced, distributed, or transmitted in any form or by any means, including photocopying, recording, or other electronic or mechanical methods, or by any information storage and retrieval system without the prior written permission of the publisher, except in the case of very brief quotations embodied in critical reviews and certain other noncommercial uses permitted by copyright law.

Contents

Chapter 1: Who We Are

Chapter 2: Exclusive Member Benefits

Chapter 3: Selection Criteria

Chapter 4: Intrinsic Value of LOD Membership

Chapter 5: Attorney Search Feature

Chapter 6: Increase Web Traffic on a Consistent Basis

Chapter 7: Member Announcements, News and Case Results

Chapter 8: See What Members Are Saying

Chapter 9: Most Frequently Asked Questions (FAQ)

Chapter 10: LOD is Independent

Chapter 1
Who We Are

As you all know this country is saturated with lawyers like a wet paper towel. Where do they keep coming from and how can they all survive? At this time there are roughly 1.3 million lawyers in the United States. It is perhaps the most crowded profession in the country. We are frequently asked how a lawyer can get some exposure and enhance their law firms prestige without a $100,000 or $500,000 advertising/marketing budget?

In order to answer this question, we looked into pay per click advertising (too expensive for legal search terms) as well as good old-fashioned SEO (law firms have full time employees optimizing). So, how does a small to medium sized firm or solo practitioner increase their organic search results? We have found that lawyers who are members of vanity legal organizations frequently outrank their local competitors. This is because Google, as well as other search engines, recognize these lawyers as having a particular expertise. These lawyers are then clicked on and searched more often which then begins a cycle causing rankings to steadily increase.

So, how can membership in Lawyers of Distinction (L.O.D.) benefit my reputation? Part of the answer is definitely the strength of the Lawyers Of Distinction logo and branding both online and in all professional materials.

What else does L.O.D. do for Members that differentiates them from other legal vanity organizations? Lawyers of Distinction is unique amongst Lawyer Marketing companies insofar as they publicize member names through press releases, online announcements, and on social media (Facebook and Twitter) year round. Members are each publicized nationally through the New York Times, A.B.A. Journal, and numerous other outlets both in print and online. Through these multiple channels, Members are actively promoted both to the legal community as well as to the general public. This multi-pronged approach provides members far and away the best bang for the buck for their marketing dollars.

For 2018, L.O.D. has implemented a new feature whereby potential clients can directly search for and retain quality representation. Presently, thousands of people visit the website directory daily! Unlike most competitors, Lawyers of Distinction does not refer clients to specific attorneys and therefore is not a lawyer referral service. Lawyers cannot pay for greater placement or banner ads, etc. This creates a unique user experience whereby one can search for a lawyer geographically or by specialization or both, making informed consumer decisions.

Lawyers of Distinction provides exclusive member benefits at a very reasonable price As of this writing membership options begin at $475.00.

This is just the beginning. To learn more about our exclusive Member Benefits and our "Member Discount Program" continue to Chapter 2.

Chapter 2
Exclusive Member Benefits

Are you ready to take your law practice to the next level? Once membership has been approved, Lawyers of Distinction Members will receive comprehensive benefits unrivaled by any other legal organization.

Included in Membership are the following benefits:

-A custom genuine wood plaque and/or a translucent glass crystal stating membership.

-Inclusion within the exclusive Lawyers of Distinction Directory. Thousands of people use the directory daily in search of competent representation in over 20 areas of practice, both civil and criminal. A Directory listing includes member name, practice area, website link, address, headshot, social media and biographical information.

-Use of the Lawyers of Distinction licensed Logo on their website and other promotional materials.

-Membership Roster announcements in The New York Times, The American Bar Association Journal, Trial Magazine, and many others.

-Online Member announcements published year-round on USA Today, Fox News, CNN and The Huffington Post websites.

-Access to a "Private Members Only Facebook Group." Each member is part of a network of attorneys thousands strong who can find attorneys in other areas of the country for referrals, co-counsel relationships, sharing of experts, case strategies and the like.

-A customized press release for the member's use and publication for both online use (website or social media blog) as well as in print.

- Annual member discounts of $5,000 dollars or more through our "Member Discount Program." Based on our size and the quality of our Members, National vendors include Avis, Hertz, Marriott, Hilton and Southwest Airlines, as well as many many others, have negotiated significant savings opportunities for Members. See a sample of these discounts below:

- Discounted gift card bundles at popular restaurants in your community

- Up to 35% off movie tickets at AMC, Regal Entertainment, and more

- Discounts on general admission pricing at over 150 national attractions

- Save up to $25 at Sam's Club, Free Products from Costco & Up to 10% off on Target.com

- Member Discounts at over 63,000 hotels

- Up to $500 off new & pre-owned cars from over 10,000 participating dealers

- 20% off flowers from over 9,000 participation florists

- Up to $75 off cable services plus free upgrades

- 15%-25% off men's and women's apparel purchases

Chapter 3
Selection Criteria

Are you ready to take your law practice to the next level? Lawyers of Distinction is a private organization that acknowledges lawyers in the United States who have demonstrated excellence in the practice of law. Members may be nominated by their peers, chosen by our Selection Committee or can nominate themselves. See the flowchart below which describes the entire Selection Process:

SELECTION PROCESS

Nominations

How a Lawyer Enters the candidate pool:
- Nominated by peers or completion of online application
- Third party feedback
- Identified by Lawyers of Distinction selection committee

Independent Research

Evaluation on indicators of professional achievement & peer recognition:

- Experience
- Honors/Awards
- Case Results
- Verdicts/Settlements
- Special Certifications
- Representative Clients
- Professional Activities
- Educational Background
- Pro Bono & Community Service
- Scholarly Lectures/Writings
- Other Outstanding Achievements

No individual factor is given undue weight Lawyers of Distinction seeks diversity amongst its members

Ethics Review & Background Check

Candidates must not have any ethics violations in the past 10 years.

Final Selection

All attorneys who have met our standard are then accepted for membership. Lawyers of Distinction shall not confirm membership to more than 10% of attorneys in any given state.

Chapter 4
Intrinsic Value of LOD Membership

Recently, lawyer marketing/vanity organizations have come under attack. Are they legit? The attacks have come predominantly from jealous outsiders looking in and legal marketing companies who often times have their own agenda. The answer is a resounding YES. Lawyers of Distinction is absolutely transparent in our selection process. Lawyers of Distinction allows other attorneys to nominate peers or the candidate may be selected by the Selection Committee. Lastly, Lawyers of Distinction allows self-nomination.

Some critics challenge the objectivity of such selection criteria. The reality is that this is a platform for information and a starting point for the public. In this way, Lawyers of Distinction is a valuable resource to those in need of competent legal representation.

Others complain that the selection or nomination of attorneys is entirely subjective. Well, first of all for the aforementioned reasons it certainly is not. More importantly, these critics fail to realize that L.O.D. Members are a very highly educated and sophisticated group of people. You know exactly why you are joining and how Membership can give your practice some practical tools to thrive in a highly competitive legal environment.

The proof of customer satisfaction is the explosive growth of L.O.D. and the fact that 95% of our Members renew.

Chapter 5
Attorney Search Feature

For 2018, L.O.D. has implemented our newest feature whereby potential clients can directly search for and retain quality representation. Unlike most competitors, Lawyers of Distinction does not refer clients to specific attorneys and therefore is not a lawyer referral service.

Lawyers cannot pay for greater placement or banner ads, etc. This creates a unique user experience whereby prospective clients can search for a lawyer geographically or by specialization or both, making informed consumer decisions as opposed to contacting the next Johnny come lately on television. At the time of publication of this book, more than 5,000 unique users visit the website daily in search of representation. This trend will only accelerate as we continually reinvest dollars into marketing L.O.D. to the general public.

Chapter 6
Increase Web Traffic on a Consistent Basis

L.O.D.'s team of search engine optimizers stay continually at the cutting edge of the latest changes to Google algorithm's. The last three major Google algorithm updates are known as Hummingbird, Panda, and Penguin. Our engineers use this technology so that your personal profile page is expertly optimized. Below is a brief description of these algorithms:

Hummingbird was designed to pay more attention to individual words in a search query, so the overall meaning of the query is considered. The results are that sites that match the whole meaning of a query do better than sites that match only a few words of a query.

Panda was designed to prevent sites with poor quality from finding their way into the top of search results.

Lastly, Penguin was designed to catch sites that were spamming the search results by buying backlinks or getting them through link networks designed to boost search rank.

Chapter 7
Member Announcements, News and Case Results

Upon acceptance, each Member receives a custom "Press Release" generated by L.O.D. and emailed to our Member. The press release can be used in so many ways. Lawyers have sent it for publication to their local media, firm newsletters, website announcements, blogs, social media and many other creative ways.

L.O.D. also publishes a welcome email announcement on the Lawyers of Distinction Facebook page as well as Twitter.

We encourage Members to provide us with any news stories, professional announcements, case results or other newsworthy stories. Upon editorial review, we then will publish this information on our website blog, on Facebook, and in our Monthly Newsletter.

As you can see we are with you all the way, here to help you stand out all year long.

CHAPTER 8
SEE WHAT MEMBERS ARE SAYING

- Khambrel Davis, Esq. "Lawyers of Distinction membership has been one of the smartest things I've done in my law career. They have delivered on everything they have promised. The discounts alone have made up for the cost of membership. I would highly recommend Lawyers of Distinction to other attorneys."

-Khambrel Davis, Esq. "Joining Lawyers of Distinction has been one of the most lucrative decisions I have made for my practice thus far. The network of elite attorneys is only one of the advantages you receive as a member, that coupled with the other amazing benefits I gained has grown my firm to an amount I never thought was scalable in such a short period of time. Needless to say, I highly recommend Lawyers of Distinction."

-Siavash Tourzani, Esq. "I really love the plaque I received. Many clients comment on it and compliment me and it looks beautiful hanging with my other diplomas and awards. Thank you!"

-Rolando Sanchez, Esq. "I am so flattered to have been selected for membership and Lawyers of Distinction. I think the directory is awesome and I have seen an increase in my new cases directly through online searches. I will highly recommend LOD to anyone who wants to grow their practice."

-Matthew Sosnick, Esq. " The Lawyers of Distinction organization has been a huge catalyst for my firm. The exposure of membership and the opportunities to leverage this honor has been great for my practice."

-Tiffany Feder, Esq. "Lawyers of Distinction is a wonderful organization. It creates a forum where the finest of attorneys are recognized."

-Jason Mark, Esq. " I really appreciate the attention to detail of the membership plaque. I have received multiple compliments. The press release was fantastic and it has been posted and reposted several times on Facebook. Thanks LOD"

CHAPTER 9
MOST FREQUENTLY ASKED QUESTIONS (FAQ)

-Does Membership Require Recommendations From Other Attorneys? No, members are evaluated based upon peer recognition, reputation, and past results.

-How will I be able to use trademarked materials? During your annual membership term, you may freely use the Lawyers of Distinction logo on your letterhead, law firm pamphlets, and mailing materials as well as print media and other forms of advertising. Members may also use the logo and other trademarked materials on their website.

-How long is membership valid? Membership is valid 1 year from acceptance of an application.

-How long will it take to receive my plaque and welcome materials? Materials will be received in 4-6 weeks.

-What is the Lawyers of Distinction selection process? Lawyers may become members by invitation, nomination, or direct application.

-Does Lawyers of Distinction accept all types of lawyers? Yes, Lawyers of Distinction accepts lawyers from the following practice areas: Bankruptcy, Corporate and Transactional, Criminal Defense, Disability and Workers Comp, Employment & Labor Law, Estate Planning – Wills & Trust, Family & Divorce, Immigration, Intellectual Property – Patents, Trademarks, Copyright &

Licensing, Mediation, Personal Injury, Real Estate & Property, Civil Litigation. Lawyers of Distinction may add additional practice areas upon request.

-How can I change the information displayed in my online profile? Please e-mail us directly at jesse@lawyersofdistinction.com to change the information on your profile.

-How do I nominate a lawyer? Simple click here and fill out the required information.

-How do I order additional plaques? Please e-mail jesse@lawyersofdistinction.com to request an additional plaque.

-What is a featured attorney? Featured attorneys have an upgraded level of membership. "Featured Attorney" membership includes exclusive & prominent placement on the website, member e-mails & advertisement.

-What is a distinguished attorney? Distinguished attorneys have an upgraded level of membership. "Distinguished Attorney" membership includes exclusive & prominent placement on the website, member e-mails & advertisement. It also is the only level of membership that includes the 11″ tall translucent personalized crystal statue.

-How do I cancel my membership? To cancel your membership please email jesse@lawyersofdistinction.com 30 days prior to your renewal.

CHAPTER 10
LOD IS INDEPENDENT

Lawyers of Distinction members have been selected based upon a review and vetting process from our Selection Committee. After a thorough review of credentials, attorneys are nominated by our Selection Committee. Lawyers do not pay for this nomination. These potential candidates who meet the criteria of our screening process have demonstrated a high degree of peer recognition and professional competence. Attorneys may nominate other peers they feel warrant recognition or self-nominate. These candidates undergo the same rigorous review process. Lawyers of Distinction uses its own independent criteria, including both objective and subjective factors in determining if an attorney can be recognized as a Lawyer of Distinction in the United States in their respective field. This designation is based upon the proprietary analysis of the Lawyers of Distinction organization alone and is not intended to be endorsed by any of the 50 United States Bar Associations or The District of Columbia Bar Association. Lawyers of Distinction shall not confirm membership to more than 10% of attorneys in any given state. Any references to "excellent", "excellence" or "distinguished" are meant to refer to the Lawyers of Distinction organization and not to any named member individually.

ONE LAST THING…

If you enjoyed this book or found it useful I'd be very grateful if you'd post a short review on Amazon. Your support really does make a difference and I read all the reviews personally so I can get your feedback and make this book even better.

Thanks again for your support!

www.ingramcontent.com/pod-product-compliance
Lightning Source LLC
Chambersburg PA
CBHW030111230526
45471CB00003B/1364